A Benjamin Blog and His Inquisitive Dog Guide

Brazil

Anita Ganeri

Raintree is an imprint of Capstone Global Library Limited, a company incorporated in England and Wales having its registered office at 7 Pilgrim Street, London, EC4V 6LB – Registered company number: 6695582

www.raintreepublishers.co.uk
myorders@raintreepublishers.co.uk

Edited by Dan Nunn, Helen Cox Cannons, and Gina Kammer
Designed by Jo Hinton-Malivoire
Picture research by Ruth Blair and Hannah Taylor
Production by Helen McCreath
Originated by Capstone Global Library Ltd
Printed and bound in China

ISBN 978 1 406 28108 8
18 17 16 15 14
10 9 8 7 6 5 4 3 2 1

British Library Cataloguing in Publication Data
A full catalogue record for this book is available from the British Library.

Acknowledgements
We would like to thank the following for permission to reproduce photographs:

Alamy: Greg Balfour Evans, 4, Horizons WWP, 21, imagebroker, 18, Manfred Gottschalk, cover, Paul Springett 05, 13, Photoshot Holdings Ltd., 10, Simon Reddy, 20; Getty Images: AFP, 17, Caterina Bernardi, 14, Diego Lezama, 25, FIFA/Alex Livesey, 22, Jeremy Walker, 27, John W. Banagan, 6, Latincontent/Jan Sochor, 19, Mike Theiss, 23, National Geographic, 15, Rowan Castle, 8; Science Photo Library: PLANETOBSERVER, 9; Shutterstock: cifotart, 12, Costas Anton Dumitrescu, 11, Mark Schwettmann , 29, wavebreakmedia, 28; Superstock: Hemis.fr, 7, imagebroker.net, 16, Robert Harding Picture Library, 26, Stock Connection, 24

Every effort has been made to contact copyright holders of material reproduced in this book. Any omissions will be rectified in subsequent printings if notice is given to the publisher.

Some words are shown in bold, **like this**. You can find out what they mean by looking in the glossary.

Contents

Welcome to Brazil!

Hello! My name is Benjamin Blog and this is Barko Polo, my **inquisitive** dog. (He is named after ancient ace explorer **Marco Polo**.) We have just got back from our latest adventure – exploring Brazil. We put this book together from some of the blog posts we wrote on the way.

Brazil
Topographical
Map

ATLANTIC
OCEAN

VENEZUELA
COLOMBIA
GUYANA
SURINAME
French
Guiana

Guiana
Highlands
Pico da
Nablina
Serra de
Tumucumaque

Negro River
Amazon River

Amazon Basin
Manaus

S E L V A S   A M A Z O N

PERU

Juruá River
River
Purus

Madeira River
R A I N   F O R E S T
Catingas

Fortaleza

Recife

Araguaia River
Tocantins River
São Francisco River

Xingu River

BRAZILIAN

Salvador

BOLIVIA

Planalto do
Mato Grosso

Brasília ✪

HIGHLANDS

Belo
Horizonte
Ouro Preto

Paraná River

Campos

São
Paulo

Rio de
Janeiro

N
W   E
S

0   200   400 mi.
0   200   400 k

PARAGUAY

Iguaçu R.

Serra do Mar

ATLANTIC
OCEAN

ARGENTINA

Porto
Alegre

URUGUAY

BARKO'S BLOG-TASTIC BRAZIL FACTS

Brazil is the biggest country in South America. It covers about half of the **continent**. It has a very long coastline with the Atlantic Ocean in the east.

5

Historic places

On day one of our trip, we are in Ouro Preto, a city in the southeast of Brazil. It is famous for its amazing buildings, which were built by Portuguese settlers in the 1700s. The Portuguese arrived in Brazil in 1500 and ruled the country for more than 300 years.

BARKO'S BLOG-TASTIC BRAZIL FACTS

In 1960 the capital of Brazil moved from Rio de Janeiro to the brand new city of Brasília. This is the National Congress Building.

Mountains, rivers, and rainforests

Posted by: Ben Blog | 21 October at 2.39 p.m.

Our next stop was the Pico da Neblina in the north, where I took this photo. It is 3,014 metres (9,888 feet) tall, making it Brazil's highest mountain. Its name means "misty peak," and it certainly lives up to it. According to the locals, its top is almost always in the clouds.

BARKO'S BLOG-TASTIC BRAZIL FACTS

The awesome Amazon River starts in the Andes Mountains in Peru. It flows for 6,437 kilometres (4,000 miles) across Peru and Brazil and into the Atlantic Ocean.

The biggest rainforest on Earth grows along the banks of the Amazon River. It is about the same size as Australia, and I could not wait to explore it. Some local people offered to be our guides. They have lived in the rainforest for years and know it like the backs of their hands, so I will not get lost.

BARKO'S BLOG-TASTIC BRAZIL FACTS

The Amazon rainforest is home to an astonishing number of plants and animals. In fact, about one in 10 of all known **species** live there. This colourful **toucan** was easy to spot!

Big cities

Posted by: Ben Blog | 30 December at 3.21 p.m.

We have arrived in São Paulo, the biggest city in Brazil. See the picture I took! It is home to around 18 million people, so it is a very busy place. More than three-quarters of Brazilians live in towns and cities. Brazil's second-biggest city is Rio de Janeiro, about 400 kilometres (248 miles) up the coast.

BARKO'S BLOG-TASTIC BRAZIL FACTS

The city of Manaus was built in the middle of the rainforest in the 1600s. This is the Amazonas Theatre in the city. It is built from bricks, glass, and marble brought from Europe.

13

Bom dia!

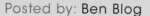

Most people in Brazil speak Portuguese. *Bom dia* means "good day" or "good morning." There are also many ancient South American languages. About 200 million people live in Brazil. Many of them have a mixture of South American, Portuguese, and African **ancestors**.

14

BARKO'S BLOG-TASTIC BRAZIL FACTS

Thousands of people, such as these Kayapo, live in the rainforest. Many still hunt animals for food and treat the forest with great care and **respect**.

In Brazil there is a big gap between the rich and the poor. Many poor people move to the cities to find work. Some end up living in **favelas** (slums), such as this one in Rio de Janeiro. The houses are made from tin or wood, and there are no toilets, running water, or electricity.

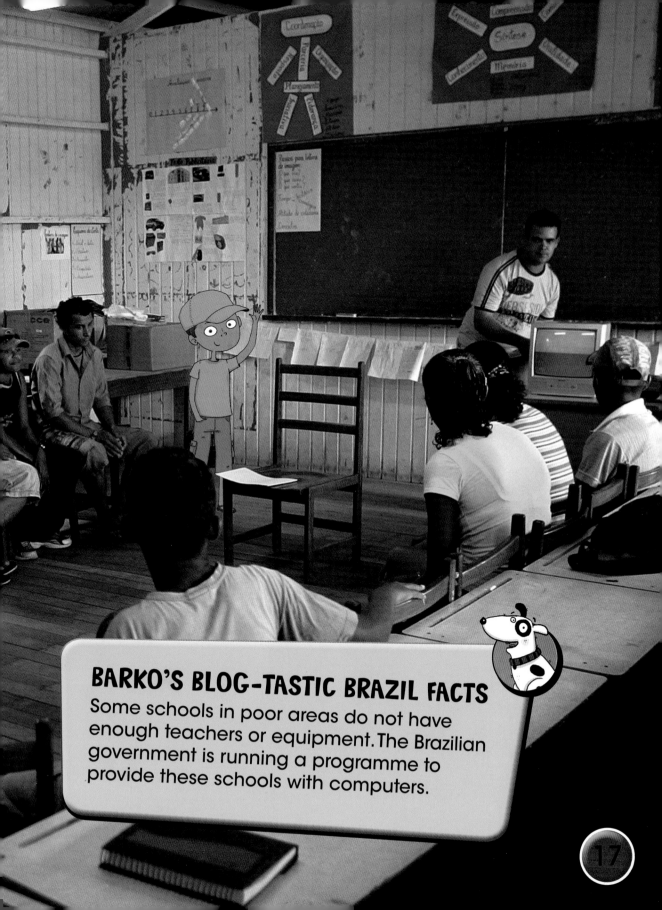

BARKO'S BLOG-TASTIC BRAZIL FACTS

Some schools in poor areas do not have enough teachers or equipment. The Brazilian government is running a programme to provide these schools with computers.

We are staying in Rio because it is Carnival time – the highlight of our trip! Every year, 40 days before Easter, thousands of dancers take to the streets for a spectacular show. They are dressed in fantastic costumes that take many months to make. Is that Barko with the dancers?

BARKO'S BLOG-TASTIC BRAZIL FACTS

Most Brazilians are **Roman Catholics**, but some mix Christian and African beliefs. These people are celebrating the festival of Iemanjá, the African goddess of the sea.

A bite to eat

All that dancing made us hungry, so we stopped for something to eat. I picked feijoada. It is a stew made from smoked meat and beans and served with rice. It is eaten all over Brazil. Very tasty. Barko had churrasco – pieces of meat on **skewers**, cooked over a barbecue.

BARKO'S BLOG-TASTIC BRAZIL FACTS

Rainforest people get all of their food from the forest itself. They hunt animals for meat, collect nuts, roots, and berries, and grow crops, such as **plantains** and **manioc**.

Football crazy

Posted by: Ben Blog | 3 March at 12.10 p.m..

Staying in Rio, we are off to watch a football match at the Maracanã **Stadium**. The Brazilians are crazy about football. The national team has won the World Cup a record five times. Brazil's greatest ever football player, Pelé, was a member of the team for three of those victories.

BARKO'S BLOG-TASTIC BRAZIL FACTS

At weekends, thousands of Brazilians head for the beach to surf, play beach football, and sunbathe. This is Copacabana Beach in Rio – one of the most famous beaches in the world.

From mining to coffee making

Posted by: Ben Blog | 18 April at 9.37 a.m.

From Rio, we travelled north into the rainforest, where I took this photo of the massive Carajas mine. Here, huge diggers dig up thousands of tonnes of rocks that contain valuable iron. Mining is very important in Brazil, even though large areas of the rainforest are dug up to look for iron and other minerals.

BARKO'S BLOG-TASTIC BRAZIL FACTS

Brazil grows more coffee than any other country in the world. Most of it is sold in other countries. The coffee is grown on huge farms, called fazendas, such as this one in the state of Minas Gerais.

And finally ...

It is the last day of our tour, and we stopped at the incredible Iguaçu Falls. They are between Brazil and Argentina and are 82 metres (269 feet) high and 3 kilometres (2 miles) wide. You can take a bus from the nearest town for a better view of the falls.

BARKO'S BLOG-TASTIC BRAZIL FACTS

This huge statue of Jesus Christ stands on top of Corcovado Mountain, overlooking Rio de Janeiro. The statue stands 30 metres (98 feet) tall, and its open arms stand for peace.

Brazil fact file

Area: 8,514,877 square kilometres
(3,287,612 square miles)

Population: 201,009,622 (2013)

Capital city: Brasília

Other main cities: São Paulo; Rio de Janeiro

Language: Portuguese

Main religion: Christianity (Roman Catholic)

Highest mountain: Pico da Neblina
(3,014 metres/9,888 feet)

Longest river: Amazon River
(6,437 kilometres/4,000 miles)

Currency: Real

Brazil quiz

Find out how much you know about Brazil
with our quick quiz.

1. What is the capital of Brazil?
a) Rio de Janeiro
b) Brasilia
c) São Paulo

2. Which ocean does the Amazon River flow into?
a) Atlantic Ocean
b) Pacific Ocean
c) Arctic Ocean

3. What language do Brazilians speak?
a) Spanish
b) French
c) Portuguese

4. Which is the most popular sport in Brazil?
a) football
b) baseball
c) tennis

5. What is this?

5. statue of Jesus Christ
4. a
3. c
2. a
1. b
Answers

Glossary

ancestor a relative from the past

continent one of seven huge areas of land on Earth

favela a poor, overcrowded part of a Brazilian city

inquisitive being interested in learning about the world

manioc a plant with potato-like root

Marco Polo an explorer who lived from about 1254 to 1324; he travelled from Italy to China

plantain a banana-like fruit, used in cooking

respect being polite and helpful to someone else

Roman Catholic a Christian who belongs to the Roman Catholic Church

skewer a long, pointed stick made from wood or metal, for cooking food

species a particular type of living thing

stadium a place where sports are played, with seats for spectators

toucan a rainforest bird with a large, colourful beak

Find out more

Books

Brazil (Changing World), Nicola Barber
(Franklin Watts, 2011)

Brazil (My Country), Annabel Savery
(Franklin Watts, 2014)

Spotlight on Brazil (Spotlight on My Country), Bobbie
Kalman (Crabtree Publishing, 2011)

Websites

kids.nationalgeographic.com/kids/places
The National Geographic website has lots of
information, photos, and maps of countries around
the world.

www.worldatlas.com
Packed with information about various countries,
this website includes flags, time zones, facts, maps
and timelines.

Index